D0361429

IN THE BELLY

Phoenix Poets

A SERIES EDITED BY ALAN SHAPIRO

In the Belly

DAVID GEWANTER

THE UNIVERSITY OF CHICAGO PRESS *Chicago & London*

DAVID GEWANTER teaches writing at Harvard University. His poetry and prose appear in several journals, including *Threepenny Review, Agni,* and *Ploughshares;* and in anthologies such as *New Voices Anthology* and *The National Poetry Competition* anthology. He is a consulting editor for *Tikkun.*

The University of Chicago Press, Chicago 60637
The University of Chicago Press, Ltd., London
© 1997 by The University of Chicago
All rights reserved. Published 1997
Printed in the United States of America
06 05 04 03 02 01 00 99 98 97 1 2 3 4 5

ISBN: 0–226–28872–2 (cloth)
ISBN: 0–226–28873–0 (paper)

Gewanter, David.
    In the belly / David Gewanter.
        p.   cm. — (Phoenix poets)
    ISBN 0-226-28872-2 (cloth). — ISBN 0-226-28873-0 (paper)
    I. Series.
    PS3557.E89715   1997
    811'.54—dc20
                                                    96-18329
                                                    CIP

♾ The paper used in this publication meets the minimum requirements of the American National Standard for Information Sciences—Permanence of Paper for Printed Library Materials, ANSI Z39.48-1984.

For A. P. Gewanter, M.D.

Hang there like a fruit, my soul,
Till the tree die

—Cymbeline

Contents

III   Autopsy

Acknowledgments

Several of the poems in this book originally appeared in the following publications:

AGNI: "Letter In My Desk" (1989), "Leopard Man" (1992), "The Competition" (1996), "Bill" (1990).

Berkeley Fiction Review: "The Pardon" (1988).

Berkeley Poetry Review: "Goya's *The Third of May, 1808*" (1987); "Catalunya: A Letter" (1989).

Berkeley Voice: "Early Words" (1989).

Boston Phoenix: "Three for the Organ Grinder" (1996).

Boston Review: "Boy's Poem" (1994).

Harvard Review: "*Shield*" (1994).

New England Review/Bread Loaf Quarterly: "Rock, Paper, Scissors" (1987).

Ploughshares Vol. 18, no. 4: "In the Belly," "Conduct of Our Loves" (1992).

Quinnipiac Schweitzer Journal: "My Father's Autopsy" (Winter 1994/95).

Threepenny Review: "Push Play" (1989); "The Fossil" (orig. "The Work-Towers"; 1994).

Tikkun: "English 1" (1987); "*Yeartime* for the Intifada" (1990).

TriQuarterly: "Last Garden" (Winter 1997).

"Goya's *The Third of May, 1808*" and "'Waste Ground & Weeds,'" both appear in the anthology *New Voices* (Academy of American Poets), chosen by Donald Hall, 1989. "'Waste Ground & Weeds'" may be found in *Arvon Anthology Poems* (Arvon Foundation), chosen by Ted Hughes and Seamus Heaney, 1989; "English 1" in the *Ina Coolbrith Anthology*, 1989. "Bleish the Barber" appears in *Shirim Competition*

(Intermedia Publications), chosen by Gerald Stern and Grace Shulman, 1988; and "Early Words" in *The National Poetry Competition* (Chester A. Jones Foundation), chosen by Diane Wakowski and Marvin Bell, 1986.

A book so heavy with names should spare adding more here. Thanks go to my "four fathers," great teachers and poets initialed here—F.B., T.G., S.H., R.P.—and to other friends helping these pages. "The Fossil" is dedicated to sculptor Mark Di Suvero.

Annals of the Wonder-Cabinet

O, that record is lively in my soul
　　　　　　—Twelfth Night.

The squat jars racked in the lab hold
fetuses, blunted heads adrift
in formalin—

childlings
who never lived
to their deaths, and fattened our histories

not by dying, but by "dying from ———,"
a null-word we tally on a
body bag,

pickling
fear in a technical
elegy. The man whose ankle breaks under

a too-tight sheet, who lumbers through
the monkey zoos of therapy
dropping pencils

into a cup—
then doctors come,
shrouds inspecting a shroud of origins,

to lift his smock and finger the mysteries
on a chart. The end of
a world

is simpler
than we imagine, a senile
paradise born from us thoughtlessly—

That disease survives the body
equates it with the soul,
for whom life

is illness
—so Socrates proclaimed,
his legs numbing to the groins. The State drips

Texas Mix into the arm, three lethal doses
for man of body, mind, soul:
end of sentence

and narrative.
The causes of dying
forge an endless chainsong, whispered reasons

or lies for foot-drag, flinch, his slack eye
watching the nurse's button—
"The king died

and the queen died
from grief" we add, or hear
"the clock of cancer tick in the body"

of a poem. Minds powerless to heal can dream up
life—Dr. Fleming, bored, dabs a
petri dish with

bacteria—a portrait
of his mother, brown hair
of proteus, *E. coli* skin, while from vents

the spores of penicillin pass, *mind upon the waters,*
and blot the cameo green.
He frowns, seeing

her ruined
by the new world, wondering
vaguely . . . and so the dead continue to swell,

each death a failed hypothesis, the spongy
hatchling in a brain
unread

by doctors,
who ask the withered man
instead what letters they trace on his arm—

tapping him, counting his sugars, waiting
until his Rushmore head cracks
open their report.

I   **SHIELD**

In the Belly

Dad pays him to teach me the boy thought
as the old man watched from behind jib—
The cool burnt cherry from his pipe

sweetened the ocean smell, its spoilage
and cure of brine. On tack or coming about,
the man was practical, oracular:

Weight the gunwale on close hauls. Don't luff.
He read out the lesson while the boy
turned the page of the sail. One day

a leeward chill brought the man's eyes
down to his wet lap: *Jesus. Son, sit athwart.*
He took the sheet, and the boom swung

like a dowser to the wind. *He's older
than Grandpa; he'll die soon* the boy thought,
watching the piss eddy near his feet.

On pier the old man stumped off. The boy
wandered around, he found a giant kettle
"From the last whaling ship, 1860"

looming like a monster's egg. The charred
candlefat iron stung his eyes. He'd read about
boiling blubber, "A reeking soup of flesh . . ."

But this, the stink left in the belly
of the pot, this was new: it was not
of the sea, not of the old man's piss—

Leaning in, he squinted at genitals and names,
at what a century of boys had dared
to scrawl inside the passive flank.

English 1

FIRST, We tied to each other
NEXT, Coconuts for the swimming
THEN, The Boat-Soldiers shoot
MEANWHILE, Many dying
AND THEN, We swam with dead People
LATER, We get on the land
FINALLY, We left our dead Friends.

What grade does this exercise deserve?
Homework folded like a handkerchief,
a little book of tears, burns, escape—

And still I mark the blasphemies
of punctuation, common speech;
the English tune will help them live.

Rickety Hmong boy, flirting simply
with the loud girl from Managua—
I taught him how to ask her out,

taught her how to say no, nicely;
my accent and suburban decorums
are tidy and authoritative as

the checks I make for right answers,
the rosy golf-clubs on the page.
By next year they'll talk their way

out of trouble instead of smiling
as they do hearing me drone *Silent Night*—
They join in, shy and hypnotized,

Saigon chemist, cowed Haitian, miming
the words I once told my music teacher
that Jews shouldn't sing: "Holy Infant."

Yeartime for the Intifada

At dusk, Jerusalem glows like a nursery tale,
windows lit for its lost children.
Other boys and girls play in the alleys—
one tosses a rock straight up for joy

like a firework before it bursts;
tomorrow he'll heave a brick,
project of his life—

Among the spices on my shelf, this cup of wax:
a *Yartzeit* candle, for marking a death-day;
which grandparent's, I forget. *Yeartime.*
The dictionary gives rhymes for pronouncing it,

Dart site (German)
Court site (Yiddish);
a huddled joke about Aryans and Jews—

The boy throws a rock straight up for joy
(like a missile at Hofburg, aimed at tanks
rolling across its own silo). . . . Tomorrow
his parents will hold his body and weep.

The spirit of man is a candle of God
—in a Proverb. But the boy dreamed
his wick would burn so God could see him. . . .

Nipple, leaking its fuel—
he might caper in the flame this year
if a candle is set, if that
is how his people celebrate their dead.

The Pardon

for Ezra Pound

Jew and Jew-hater, fingers stretched
round each other's throat, wheeze
their intimate threats in this
unending heaven of rhetoric

I see behind his book—and he
might have joined that bickering chorus
once his body sloughed off
and left him breathing in his own mask,

one, many-voiced . . . but he died
renouncing his "suburban prejudice"—
denying the purity of his hate.
Since then, the metal starfish of fame

has grown around his head:
each new opinion mottles the crust,
already burred and sticky with topics.
Neither words nor silence can

crack it open—my hands reach in,
feeling for the face crammed somewhere
inside: confused, sour, intractable,
denying me the fullness of revenge.

And so he is pardoned of authority:
he cannot enter this Garden of Enemies
and bear the judgment of my embrace—
the self-annulling reverence demanded by his book.

Goya's The Third of May, 1808

I'll show you:
onto the dirt-grey
canvas he's smeared—
jam on bread—
a sticky red for blood
oozed from the broken
heads and shot-up bodies
heaped near the cowering group
agape at soldiers hunched above
their knived rifles.
The air is oil-black,
smokeless, the whole scene
painted right before the guns
report, and more killed;
see the soldiers bend
in careful aim, bent
like mothers nursing—
one geometry of care:
exact angle for Madonna,
for men aiming murder—
and yet suspended,
the crisis held up for us
to observe at leisure—
in *The Resurrection* by
Grünewald, think how Christ
has bolted from his tomb,

rising, splendid,
while blinded soldiers
hurl themselves down,
never landing—
all are trapped in place:
one can't reach heaven,
the others never fall—
and here, before the dull wedge
representing *hill,*
one of Goya's victims
raises his arms up,
waiting always—
you know him, his shirt
blank as a page—
here, hand me a butterknife
to scrape with, I'll show you how
he painted bullets
inside the painted guns.

Letter In My Desk

Dear David,
Not writing back seems a *conscious* act—
maybe you've been too busy, whatever;
    or you got suspicious

    after my last letter
and talked to my folks. I worry about that,
and then I worry about worrying.
    I'm sorry I lied

    in the letter.
This "campus" is a psychiatric institution
—it's as ugly as that sounds.
    I'm sorry.

    When you wrote,
I knew our boyhood interest in Creativity
continued. I feel like we're moving in some
    sort of parallel

    to each other
but didn't realize, like a dream
I had where a man was following me
    in front.

    My doctor says
I'm an exceptionally complex person.
Rereading this, I know it's all jumbled—
    They give me

psychotropic drugs
to block "attacks," then others to block
the side effects. By the evenings
    I can hardly walk.

    Some people here,
they just lift them up and down with drugs,
like puppets. They say I won't be able
    to do math anymore—

    cure or side effect?
What exactly am I being saved *for*.
I know an ex-patient who's going
    to sue these doctors

    for what they've done.
I'm writing you early before the drugs hit.
I can explain how this has happened—
    but not why.

    Remember Mrs. Claxton
who had the hate-vein in her forehead?
(That's when we secretly wore weight-vests
    under our sweaters

    and squeezed balls
to build ourselves up.) She'd tell us
"Complete your sentences" and we'd joke
    about prison terms.

Well, reading a lot
in college sometimes, a phrase or sign
gave other meanings, coded messages to me.
        Someone would say

        "I'm a twin"
and I'd realize everything that meant . . . Or
seeing your name sliced up in a birthday cake.
        Or the sign

WATCH REPAIRS.
It's stupid I know—but in a way,
it's an *order*. Or this sequence in the
        Penguin Dictionary:

        kourbash - Egyptian whip
        kowtow - bow down in China
        kraal - fenced in S. Africa
        krait - venomous Indian snake
        kraken - sea-monster, North Sea
        Kremlin - . . . !!

        I made connections,
under-systems they wouldn't show us in school.
Learning a career was just learning to adjust
        a machine that's

        grinding us up.
I got more involved in these researches—
I let school go— There's a grammar
        motivating things

we have to say.
My Doctor tells me these are all "symptoms"
of other problems; but *this* fits my theory
of interior structures

like a true statue
whose organs are carved inside the torso.
Then I had a "crisis"—actually, I was showing
how erased writings

"left" on a blackboard
were interpolated in a Professor's lecture:
A simple prolepsis. Now they tell me
it will take a while

before I can leave
or go to school part time. I can't explain
my discoveries to my parents—
you know my mom—

she cries a lot,
so I can't talk to them. I must
publish these findings, but with the drugs
I can't work long;

they net me in.
Can you help me in this. You know why.
All these years, I've been banging
on a door—

but I'm the door;
remember that Ellison phrase "Perhaps in
lower frequencies I speak for you."
Maybe I make you

afraid of me—
But even this typewriter holds the inner grid.
Three consecutive keys that form questions
       about you and me.

    Y U? I?
Your friend,

         —.S

Boy's Poem

Reverence is a part of fear.
—Plato, *Euthyphro*

His name wasn't Jack LaLanne—but close.
Lean, lazy, a drawling ironist older than us,
sauntering backfield while we ran like zealots

beneath the hope of his pass. He smoked dope
in the basement—till his dad called in a cop,
who arrested him right there. Then they drafted him:

suddenly stricken, he tried to build up his asthma,
trudging in wool round the damp fields after dinner.
But he got healthier; and they took him. We heard

he became a sniper, and with confused pride
we assured each other that he was "the best at it."
Playing full court next July, we saw him stroll up

in fatigues and boots; nobody said much, but we
shared the benediction of power-handshakes.
Next game he covered me—I was so parched

my armpits were foaming this weird jizz,
but I spun like Earl the Pearl, dribbling
"betwixt and behind," tapping almost above the rim.

At point game I hitched him right, then dabbed
down the lane—an easy hoop. Halfway through
my tomahawk he hammered me sideways, and I got up

seeing him clomp off with the ball. He bulled down
the lane and stretched toward the hoop, but low, the
long floating jump of a man who's lost his spring.

The ball was lost in a canopy of arms, there was
a ragged scrum at the key and then the ball
skittered toward me like a righteous answer

and we won. I couldn't complain or celebrate—
He wasn't playing a game. I took off,
and saw him only once after that: standing in

Friendly's Ice Cream counting his change, his head
bent over his hand like his own palm reader,
a thoughtful fake suburbanite, a vault of motives. . . .

Later I heard he went back, moving in trees
or ditches, silencing households.
I began to forget him that fall,

but the milky comfort of my victory welled
within me. I skipped football and saved
my knees: I was taller than Dad even,

made varsity, and started. And when I jumped
they gave me new names, they called me
Reindeer and Blitzen, they called me

Geewee and York and Thor, I dunked
golf balls and skewed myself toward the glass,
dustdevils at my heels as I leapt cleanly.

The Competition

4th day of fever—
fever worked its heavy belt
tighter round my head, I squinted seeing
a boy on his bike toil uphill—
toy of his youth

winding down as
earth hauled against his legs—
the bloodwaves in my neck, I stood chattering
a morse of fever to the bathroom,
tea I sipped

sapping out piss;
I curled into bed, and sleep—I saw
a strange elliptic **O** in air, tiny, dead-white
as the dot left after TV, but
swelling large

until the specks
circling it took shape, dimension—
in the passive clarity of fever I watched
cyclists languorously wheel around
this velodrome—

details grew rich:
an infield workshop, bike carcasses
rummaged from the track, skinny men hunched
over stationary frames like lovers,
running their feet

round in stirrups
while others took notes, or stared
in paranoia at the racers now pedalling the course
with agonizing lethargy, weaving up
and down the banks—

I knew a judge's bell
would clang them into sprinting
the last lap, so the fastest man could power
himself along the route he left,
and win a prize for

following himself—
but this group had almost stopped;
I tried to warn them, open my mouth inside
this dome my head made—yet as I
heard the idea

of my voice,
a bike slipped from the upper lip,
bike and biker skidding sideways down the planks
and onto the infield, as if
a flying

machine collapsed
of its weight, when the magic string
hoisting it up on a spinning wing was snapped.
The loop blacked out at his fall,
leaving a fresh

rind of fever
damp on my lifting face: day 5—
the pale curtains billow like a parachute
over my health, this morning
of my 31st year.

Shield

Aeneas delighted in these images, carved
by Vulcan on the shield his mother gave him;
joyful, distracted by the pictures,
ignorant of the events themselves, the
glory and doom of his race—he hoists it
up onto his shoulder.

Aeneid, VIII.729–731.

II CONDUCT OF OUR LOVES

Our hidden God would sooner kill us
than blind us with His glorious nature;
Beauty seals Him safe from His foundlings.

—Francisco de Medrano

A Prayer for Theft

At dawn our bedroom windows split
    Saint Someone
or other, the church across the street,

into fragments, Corinthian column, Attic attic,
    the stone fathers
spalled and dripnosed by the stairs, who watched

the tobacco shop where wise guys played
    The Godfather
on Thursdays, and cried at the murders. Under

the beef-lamps of the church, a grimy
    wattle and porcelain
crêche haloed the three silent boys

who jumped the railing and grabbed baby Jesus,
    His fat Hand blessing
from a coat as they ran. Joseph, impotent, teetered

at the crib, a virgin father keeping *omerta*. . . .
    That year Joseph
became *padrone* of the childless marriages:

the redeyed couples haunting the clinics,
    the no-fathers
sent to the salt rooms for ejaculate,

the no-mothers lined like votives, vials of
    froth in hand,
mouth tasting of clay from tests and shots and tests—

That year God's Increase groaned everywhere,
    in flower-choked
bonemeal gardens nursed day and night for

follicles of phlox, impatiens, and hosta,
    echo-plants
for broken hope: *flux, frustration, rage.*

No simples or cures here, just the sickness of
    an only life
and doctors stirring a witch-brew jelly—

Conception outside the body. Abomination unto
    Joseph's God.
Padrone, may they steal a life

from heaven, where the present is frozen. . . .
    The Mafia searched
the snows for the Babe, then trudged indoors

and wept for Fredo. By June the *festa* came,
    and lovers strapped
to the Ferris wheel held themselves above the church.

We flew to Italy, married in a palace velveted
    whorehouse red,
and played Uffizi under the sheets.

Darling girl, you drawled *La Belle Dame* in
    the voice of Elvis
as I dozed and woke up laughing—

our love so childlike but bringing
   no child.
Stir our names in the soil:

What we can be penetrates what we are.

Catalunya: A Letter

Once, during the time we were only friends,

I lived near the Parque Güell, its dirt playground a tabletop
pillared on a hundred stilts; and nearby, the coxcomb steeple
of Gaudi's incomplete *La* *Sagrada,* masted from the nave's
hooped keel. (I draw this all on glass; you see its opposite
outlined.) In stand-up bars, even auto mechanics drank
Catalan champagne at breakfast. Saturdays, that year we wrote

or didn't write, I'd shadow my meandering avenue
down to the *barrio gótico,* where the blind and crippled
hawked the daily Lotteries, and sighted men lingered
and eddied like old fish. Behind the beggar of two voices

pleading by the Market door, olives—dark as opals, brimming
over the vats—and here, see the huddled squid, figs dried
into tongues, tangled elvers, luxurious carpets of tripe,
garlands of peppers or garlic —a goat-head, noosed, its nostrils
hooked by a dangling cup into which the flavor dripped.

Here you're as rich as your hunger. Listen to the shop women:
they ask, "*¿Qué mes, reina?*" "What more, my Queen?"

We thought we loved each other well enough. We never thought
about what we wouldn't say. And like now, there were others.

You wrote me from New York you were the last nurse of the dying;
your goat-men called for you, you said you fled them, or didn't.

I saw the alley women scuff their boot-heels on the cobbles
and talk behind hands here, and in Girona, Llafranc, Port-Bou,
the cities of refuge. *Cátala,* *Catalunya*—the proud, regained
accents broke like gunbursts and echoes of gunbursts.
The night of Tejero's coup, every channel showed Laurel & Hardy
until the King came on. Wandering home, I faced you again
in that gaze you gave me once my intricate love; desire glowing
from other eyes, lidded, wide set, her face hemmed in a man's
hugging shoulder slope.

Formula

I find the right rack
in the store. My jars are here,
potent letters B-3 B-2.

Be two
I once wrote,
be with me;

you chose him—
triangles jabbing me
amo   amas   amat

love-charm
Star of David
hung from my neck.

From the Circle of Lovers

One, two, and three lovers want you
    Who's next?
One siphons your tears in secret
One licks you like a fetish
The last one yowls, dog on a scent
Each hoards your question marks of hair
    Who's next?

           •

—I left that note for you, then loafed
through the Guggenheim, ribboned
with Picasso's last orgies;
he's drawn them bushy black
or spare as my chest hairs
left on your chest;
impotent knights and scribblers
watch the action—along with me,
who know how to hide
jealousy in judgment, strolling
the circle of lovers
toward his ancient face—

           •

I see your eyes when you sleep, when I sleep.

.

Kudu and musk-ox, timber wolves
loping through the snows
of the Museum of Natural History . . .

Münch said he heard the scream
in nature—but for a boy of eight,
this was wilderness.
I walk through my anger in it,
stomach sloshing its gasoline—
On the Planetarium's
scales of Saturn, the needle
trembles at my weight.

The Abortion

They lay still as leaves between pages.
She found his shape loitering
in a woodland bled of all colors.
She woke; his shape felt new and strange.

He dreamt they were plastic statues
turning in the Science Hall—
children pushed buttons
and the loins flared pink and blue.

After the test, they'll regret
all this: each act will turn moral,
remembered, dismembered, and infused
with bile, hard motives running

beneath the love-hold
they now sanctify with secrets,
the "first shy talk" when
innocence resigned from their eyes;

and today they walk in dumb joy
along the beach—a family outing—
here, shining things shadow grief,
and all that waves have loaned to land:

rags and toothpick bones, bladders sodden
as shucked condoms which he steps on
tracing the watermarks. They whisper
a love-cause for it, they read their love

in everything, in details of sunlight,
in allegories for waves:
he says "They unfold like these—"
his fingers unclench from his fist.

She tucks his hand inside her blouse
and smooths his neck until the hairs
tingle like iron filings. Kisses
set a new charge below, and spark

the sundering fuse, a sentence
not served out in words.

Leg-of-Mutton Pond

Through the evenings they all stroll there,
the boys whose eyes invite and dare,
they only glance, they never stare.

Above these sentries wandering slow
the leaves have stripped their husks, and grow
from plane trees posted in their rows.

A Caesar came to this new world
to search the Pond for shells and pearl—
dark at the shore, two bodies curl.

I crouch so I can spy unseen;
I crouch from what the glances mean
and what my answer could have been.

London, 1980.

Three for the Organ-Grinder

his Tyrolean mustaches, tin cup,
bellhop monkey, and box—
   Inside twists

the body of a song. Whose is it?
Once it was a poem, but a singer
   chopped out

the words and put in her own.
A painter swirled it *Starry Night*
   then ate

his paints. Whose now?
A poet carved it in terza rima.
   Oh! if we could

start over, he recited to me once
in Copy-Rite, breaking a spine to
   copy a book,

breaking a law of origins . . .
(As if the world could begin anew
   with God gone.)

One day, a man ground a meal
a boy fed his father, who choked,
   caught pneumonia,

bled from medicines, and died.
Which of them authored the death?
    (This too is my story.)

Fading, his father smiles at
the joke about Lincoln: "Lincoln:
    the man,

the car, the tunnel, the log—"
The log becomes a dead-man
    anchoring

a wall. The boy is named
remainder-man in the will.
    Each song

is a burden. The grinder,
the end-man, hauls his
    box away.

"Waste Ground & Weeds"

This year, old Aunt Miriam's first frantic hug—
"Come, Davadl!"—feels weaker and more urgent
as I'm backed against her Cancer Society sign—
Her plastic chairpad gasps for air, undents

itself till she unsqueezes me and sits again,
chopping a cabbage into confetti for her
ten-thousandth cole slaw, while the cushion
surrenders its spirit in a familiar *fferhf*. . . .

Paterson, though scholars bugle themselves blue
on its fame, an old growth pitting the nose
of New Jersey; to me, just Miriam's home—
where she's shrinking: her leg-flesh in support hose

has fallen and folded over her ankles
like the wobbly downfall of glass in its pane;
the lifeload of gravity pulls at her spine
till now she can hardly hug above my hips,

while I could rest my elbows on her head.
We use mincing knives to work the onions over,
tapping at the wood like two competing judges.
I beg off from beetcleaning and take cover

in the hall—hushed centerpin of the house,
the dead's gallery: mother's grandmother,
a flat-faced Sitting Bull in a babushka;
grim, flouncy toddlers ignoring each other

beneath the sparkling threat of a chandelier;
three lookalikes of the Serbian Assassins;
her last husband, the indefinable Felbah;
Skippy, the only smiler, who fell in

a sewer and yapped like a phantom from
Dog-Hell. I feel their eyes' dark appraisal—
we've all seen what I've done here—the little whip
of memory flicks, I hustle through the hall,

through the shrouded parlor of antique abstract
art, and over to the vinyl Vibracouch,
where in my first flushed year I hid
an ancient foldout. Is it . . . yes, intact—

I reopen her in the quiet of the bathroom—
How wrinkled she's become: creases are lashed
across her sucked-in stomach, and rat the hairdo
shaped to resemble Eisenhower's helmet;

that dark mark on her thigh—bruise or cancer?
How I boiled for her, the inviting always-never
of her lips and nipples, how briskly I answered
them in blotch after blotch of waste magic

gobbed from the life-bags, my mind broken
into visions of copulation on trapeze,
clutching bodies sewn together, or strapped
to the Vibracouch; blushblood spouts in my cheeks,

memory replaying the irreparable reel
of always-never, of when I was caught
kidnapping a harem of magazines
and ran here, pissing hard to drown her talk

of me: "If he wanted, he could see me
naked." Above the bowl, the pinned-up poster
"Waste Ground & Weeds," now bleached the milky blue
of veins under skin. Its names sound like misheard

smut: *Redshanks, Curled Dock, Petty Spurge, Mugwort,*
a ghostly Eden of outcasts; roughstemmed
spiderings, a clutch of thistle, woolly pods,
the low armor of ivy—as if a dream

gave these corrupt orders perfect beauty.
Behind them, a diminished world of rubble-heaps,
houses, a church dome's plated breast. I tuck
away my drab sweetheart, the fevered love-keep

for whom I stained my childhood. She'll become
the big-rumped Goddess of Waste, reigning over
my assembled reliquary of misdeeds:
the failed chem test; fuck-off letters, underscored;

a scorched gas-cap; the pregnancy test-tube
photo, my tiny son-spot nestled there. . . .
I wear her frozen unashamed smile as I
retreat through the kitchen. Miriam's hunched there,

pulling the swallowed neck and organ sack
from an executed chicken—its hidden
offerings. She holds a gnarled hand toward me,
and wipes the other clean on her apron.

Conduct of Our Loves

There's a kind of sky below the ocean—
a field of starfish, turning slowly
like cogs inside
a water-watch, wound by a sea river;
the star's five fingers tremble and
reach for a clam's book of meat,
into which it will inject a sedative
and then its stomach.

In The City, escaped parrots colonize
a hilltop and breed, cackling *You want that
In a bag? More hits after this* . . .

—And how should *we* conduct our loves? Black & white
judgments still beget grays, like baptisms
of the photograph:
developer is Need, stop-bath Guilt, the fixer
Memory. Then we classify the causes,
studying the elephants' "Green Penis Disease"
till we learn it is Must. The philosopher clarifies
his mind like butter;

life dumps in raw clams, and it de-natures.
So do we love who conducts our love?
The zookeeper who earned the elephants' respect

was nicknamed "God" by the others; when Nietzsche
cracked and bellowed, his mother stuffed his mouth
with apple-bits,
and he "growled dully to himself." Emptiness
propels, beauty reels—we skip in the currents. . . .
If the Angler-fish can find a female
he attaches his jaws to her genitals:
their blood-systems unite,

his heart withers, and he degenerates into
a pulsing bag of sperm, fertilizing her
unto death. Still she swims through the vaults

of black waters, her angler glowing
from its forehead stalk of flesh: a Diogenes
barrelled by her mate
and her young, prowling in God's hunger;
as the Flounder ages he flattens, and one eye
migrates toward the other, ontogeny
posing as Modern Art, just as his name
poses him as indecisive—

nature dooms that he look up to his enemies, rained
with light; but another one, swimming, can't look down,
a waffling shadow he knows, and he calls her God.

III

AUTOPSY

And the judges must be naked too, and dead.

—Plato, *Gorgias*

Bill

Two boys grew up and got sick. The first one suffered a virus that softened the bones of his legs. First his shins felt tender and fragile; then reddish sores appeared above his ankles as bits of bone worked their way to the surface. He missed a day of school; then a week; finally his parents pulled him from the fourth grade: nearly crippled, in continuous pain, he sat at home listening to the Radio—the new modern wonder. The hospital was another wonder, cool stone and wide porticos, bigger even than his school; his mother took him there to see a doctor, who gave him a lolly.

Next week they operated, and by the spring he could run again, though his calves were now creased with scars. His mother took him back to the doctor, and there she began to cry because she couldn't pay. And the doctor said she didn't have to pay, which made her cry even more and kiss his hand, and the boy swore to them both that he'd become a doctor too, and never charge money. And he did—he skipped four grades, beat the quotas, and became a pathologist (though he did charge).

And he fathered me. The second boy I know very little about, except for how he died. His father was a doctor too, and had brought the boy in sick to his own hospital; and there he received the special care a doctor's child receives. But he died, and his father asked mine to do the autopsy. My dad showed him the results: long, interlayered crystals taken from a slit of the boy's kidney. A pink shimmer under the lens. "Crystals of the sulfa drug they kept giving him at the end," he said coolly. "They drowned him."

I wonder about this man: losing his son, he must have suffered the grief that makes the mind rage with curiosity; my father sated his curiosity, but not his rage. All he tells me now is, "The guy was a Jewish orthopedist from Seattle—he asked, and he deserved to know." And I wonder about this boy—or about his corpse; for it was his corpse that taught my father about kidneys, how they can be made to do too much by doctors, and quit, and flood the body with poisons.

This is what was done to my fat Uncle Bill, though my dad didn't know it; all he knew was that his brother had survived a heart attack but was getting worse under care, and that the whole family was phoning him to drive in and do something, anything: Bill's doctors are no good. Bill's friends are all quacks. He's getting delirious, or unconscious, he's talking all dreamy. The doctor said to prepare themselves.

Dad arrived late, and bickering with my mom (I remember; I was there). They all rushed up, DO something Pete, TALK to them. His physicians, Pete, quacks. The charts. Quack Quack. Life and death are two easy thoughts for a boy of six, who had killed Nazis and Indians the whole ride up: I sat on the bench swinging my feet and talking to my cousins while Dad fended the family off, too repressed to give them comfort, too elitist to discuss the case with anyone but doctors.

Kidneys process natural toxins from the body; my uncle's were apparently too shocked to work, and the doctors were forcing water into him to make them start up. Poisoned almost to death, his mind was cut free, and he had started babbling prophecies and visions. Bill was always a terrific talker, and this probably made Dad feel worse, uncomfortable as he is with the spontaneous and uncontrolled. But on the chart he saw what the doctors were doing; and he remembered the crystals from the boy, the special case. And he thought for a while, and then began to talk.

I like to imagine some quick nasty squabble when my father usurped authority, a scene where Dad betrayed his professional ethics for the sake of his brother, whom he never felt close to anyway. But the attending physicians were probably glad to be rid of Bill, and the squat middle-european crowd in the lobby; and glad to be rid of this clipped, uncompromising man. May the blood be on his hands.

Bill was raced to another hospital, and dried out; suddenly his kidneys started in on their own and his mind left that other place; he got well, and even started work again, conducting immense, boisterous dinners every night at home; and he gained weight until his heart burst and they found him dead at his desk.

Being so smart, my father was resented by the other boys and left on his own, and has grown into a lonely awkward man. But alienation, perhaps, has made him clearheaded; the same cold excellence that kept him from us also saved his brother's life, and turned him into my remote childhood hero.

The doctor who waived his fee gave my father a chance to be a regular boy; my father then gave up his boyhood to become a doctor. The doctor who brought his son's body in wanted to know the cause of death—not to relieve his loss, but to preserve it in knowledge. These are exchanges from choice.

But the boy who died was a victim of ignorance, and he in a way was exchanged for a few years of my uncle's life. And because I'm thankful for those years, and proud of the choice my father made, I must somehow be grateful that the boy died when and how he did.

Early Words

Dad felt the heft
of a little frosted cake,
then his big fingered left
hand shoved it in his face.

My wild joyous bark
at something so silly
as Dad making a joke
on himself. "Will he

laugh too?" I thought.
His mouth opened, but
didn't smile; he caught
some fallen goop and rubbed

it through his hair. I
laughed again, so hard
and breathless and cried
happy boy tears. "The words"

his old creamy mouth growled,
"talk or be hugged." Slot eyed,
he took another cake out,
held it by its sides

and ducked his head
down in a soft smash
like he wanted to wash
his face. Then I said

the words in my elf's
voice, so he'd stop
smearing himself
white with the slop:

drunk
Daddy drunk

Rock, Paper, Scissors

When I opened my eyes again
they both were carrying me inside
the amphitheatre—
                    Nikolai Volkoff

and Iron Sheik; I'd seen them
break heads, but they had become
gentle, swift,
             dropping me into

a seat at ringside; all around me
sat the massive fleshy spectres of
the Great Ones—
                  Dick the Bruiser,

Haystacks Calhoun, terrifying heroes
and villains of Big Time Wrestling—
now rising in applause,
                    for here,

walking down the aisle of trolley tracks
and carrying groceries up the stairs
to the ring,
            was my mother. I felt

itchy, embarrassed—the men joked
and pointed out her frumpy Cold War
bathing suit—

        holding the ropes,

The Fabulous Moolah; when Mom
stepped through and touched her hand,
a doorbell chimed,

        calming the crowd

so I could hear the huckster on the p.a.:
"Fighting out of Bleish's Barber Shop
in New Jersey,

        that hypercritical

malcontent, Ruth Leah! The Ruthless!"
There was some hooting and applause,
Sheik threw a cup—

        Mom ignored them,

setting the bag by the turnbuckle
and easing herself into a chair at
the kitchen table.

        From the back,

a low grumble and hubbub followed
Dad striding toward the apron
wearing a lab-coat—

        when he tossed it

to Johnnie Apollo I smelt formaldehyde.
"Fighting the illness of humanity,
at 18 a Phi Beta B.S.:

        Aaron P.—M.D.!"

Dad drew satisfied murmurs of assent
while two groups chanted in turn
Peter, Petrus!
      The Doc's a rock!

I wondered how they knew my folks,
for I had realized that this would be
their first fight,
      that I was seeing

composites of memories: their bodies
looked young, but their faces looked
as they do now,
      the skin a terrain

of marriage-battles. Dad sat down
at the table while the crowd clapped
and urged them on—
      in front of my seat,

Moolah and Apollo skulked in a circle,
grabbing for hand holds, headlocks.
Mom spoke first:
      "Pete? Listen to me—

I've been depressed here a lot lately,
and Miriam told me about this doctor
in Paterson—Pete?"
      But he was knotting

string around the ropes with one hand,
as Moolah caught Johnnie in a wristlock,
then a chickenwing,
      and threw him down

for a stepover toehold. "Pete, she made
an appointment for me to get—it's called
Electro-Therapy—
                         What do you think?"

Body-slam, Moolah, and another, Apollo
looks dazed, he staggers around
holding his side
                         —though I know he's faking,

know that he and Moolah really love
each other, even when they fight like this
before me—
                         And they show me love,

Apollo miraculously ducks a dropkick,
he's inspired now, he applies his special
abdominal stretch,
                         then cradles Moolah into

a sleeper-hold like a lover while Dad
stands up to shout "*Shock Therapy!*
What's with you?
                         If living with me

makes you need that, you can go back
to Paterson!" The crowd roars in triumph
and derision—
                         I turn to yell at them

but Abdul the Butcher plucks me up
and swings me over the turnbuckle
onto the canvas.
                         As I get to my feet,

my folks hop over the ropes to the floor.
Now my sister Dena and my brother Harry
are walking the gangway,
                                    escorted closely

by two toddling midget wrestlers—
The Skull Brothers snatch them up,
suplex, flying axe-handle—
                                    they're tossed

like dolls among the laughing men, as Dena
and Harry stoop into the ring with me.
Voices call out
              Rock, Paper, Scissors!

my head is clogged with the lights
and clamor—but I see Gorilla Monsoon
rising like a tower below,
                                    joining

Moolah and Apollo for a three-way
match of cut-throat. They look at us:
obviously,
              we have to give a signal

so they can start the pantomime. Yet
we're half-naked, scared; they scold us
Snap out of it!
              Hurry it up now!

and we raise our fists to play the game.
Dena makes a half-cross with fingers,
I throw my hand out flat,
                                    Harry keeps

his fist—Scissors, Paper, and Rock—
but the wrestlers won't budge: it's clear
that we must fight it out,

                       that one of us

must start the cycle and cut, cover,
or smash the other. I want to go first
but I can't fight them,

                       I just feel angry—

I fall with Gorilla Monsoon crashing
to the floor, letting his two rivals
administer leg-scissors,

                       an eye-gouge—

Yet I know that this pain is love.
As they bend to their work, I spot
my parents seated

                       beneath the glare

at ringside: Mom lies across Dad's lap,
a little white-haired girl—
I shout to them:

                       "What are the rules?

What do we do?"* I can't make them answer,
but when I recognize the intimate malice
of their embrace,

                       my flesh starts to tingle.

And now, apparently, our match has ended.
The happy crowd is bulging before
the tunnel,

                       my folks lost among them.

Harry and Dena welcome their families
into the ring, trying to chide and calm
my nephews—
                         who whoop and roll around

the mat like lunatics, as I climb down
through the ropes.

Tetragrammaton

I.

I must answer these letters my mind sees
in the lost notebook: A.P. and M.D.—
they frame our family name in his signature,
my private tetragrammaton for "father"—
and they glare like the idea of a road sign
near my burning car, until I make father
stand for the A, become our rigid playtime
colossus again, so that now my brother
and I can clutch ourselves tight as fungus
round the two trunks of his ankles, and help
my sister push him down, so as he plunges

heavily, he'll bellow as in pain, which he felt,
I'm certain, when Mantle's line drive he caught
split two of his fingers apart at the crotch.

II.

Recovery, an itch itched in every poem.
The notebook is now wholly in my head—
it was under the seat when my car was hit,
burned, blew. Unharmed and angry, I hustled home
and to the hospital to tell Dad before
he saw it on TV. His heart had been bad,
and they said that shock. . . . "Poppa Doc" lay there,
old, cored-out, fat, and draped his feelings in odd
disaster-jokes: "your juvenilia burned—
so what? Look at me—prostrate, no prostate."
And no story of mine could hurt him, not Dad.

Vines of blood and sugar swayed from his arms.
We watched the news. On the one-legged nighttable
I put the charred black coin of the gas cap.

III.

Doctors slap newborns into blurting out
the first painful vowel of the imperfect
alphabet that bodies confess in codes
to surgeons or radiologists, those
who read the living; his autopsies ciphered
another language—witch-like, he recited
the dead texts of corpses backwards, and made
his craft from the body, as I've tried now—
extracting poems from the ashes of his name.
Gin-lipped one night, he predicted his own
death by heart attack; but he was outwitted,

he survived, angry, anxious for the finish,
and wanting talk, his note sent with the proxies:
"You call yourself a writer—so write me."

My Father's Autopsy

The one he did, that is, and took me to
when I was 13. I turned as white as
the old woman lying naked there;

but as he clanked out tools I inspected her
quickly, the dead cinder of her nipples,
the stiff tuft at her crotch ("Still black?

Wouldn't it turn gray?"). Dad took stock
of her length, weight, muscle tone, telling me
or the microphone how she lived,

what made her sick. "Like being a detective,"
he said, "except I answer my own questions.
Here; touch this." But I wouldn't, and

I wanted her body to resist interrogation,
prayed weirdly she never said "aah" for a doctor.
Then he slit and sawed her down the middle—

she opened as easily as a yam, or a duffel
bag; dipping delicately in, Dad scooped
out a handful of stuff, all jumbly

like underwear from Mom's dresser. He
read her guts like a priest: probing
the tubes, slicing wafers from her heart,

so thin they would glow under lens-light—
at last she yielded him a brown pebble
which I felt between his finger and thumb;

then he put it back. Death's story, deduced from
facts hard as bone—as he talked me through it,
I could hear the joyful lift in his voice. . . .

He had little patience for his house,
its prattling unready anatomies,
his wife's "incompetent housekeeping";

at night he sat over journals and drinks,
compact, severe, inward as a microscope.
Now he's home all day waiting for the mail,

hasn't cut a corpse for years. He calls
every weekend, his news familiar
as a backache, and we talk without fear.

Once I thought my pen would open him here
like the corpse on its single pan of judgment;
but as I cover this pan with pages

he is alive on another one.

Bleish the Barber

I.

Grandpa stopped short, grabbed the broom, poked it bang! bang!
against his shop ceiling whenever my aunt
upstairs "made a wrong note." Homely, obedient,
she played scales. But my pretty child-mother sang
and danced by Grandpa's mirrors, where he snip-snipped
ear hair and nostril hair, and cocked his ear for
Miriam's piano "that I two years paid for."
The men waiting for Bleish like Ruthie—full-lipped,
a barber's girl—who has hated Miriam now
68 years. Grandpa, upright, Russian, ate
onions, did 20 knuckle push-ups a day.

Miriam cried "Too small!" when his coffin banged down
on the grave-lips. "We'll measure it," diggers answered,
and took out tape. Mom ducked away: still the dancer.

II.

Grandpa stood up, the creaky *fin-de-siècle*
vegetarian, and gave a girl his seat;
the bus lurched, his bald crabbed knobby leg buckled,
and snapped. Wheeled in the hospital, he was meat
served to germs. They burrowed through flesh a statue's
age, killed hands leathered hard by a razor strap.
When Miriam phoned, we were leaving for a wedding;
long expected grief stumbled through its paces—
our shocked "Oh no!" and then, "Oh God—the wedding!"
Our shock when the blocked coffin banged the grave-top,
when the living hair shook on his dead nape.

We recorded him once in 1962.
I pull out his small old foreign voice, spooled on tape:
"Hear me? This is Grandpa— How are you? How are you?"

III.

Cantors lurked by the roads and crowed, waving their
black books at us like ancient, lost debaters:
"Sing Kaddish—two dollar! Kaddish! Come here!"
Our string of Fleetwoods paid out, slow torpedoes
bobbing in file. Everyone began to breathe;
the diggers cuddled Grandpa in, spooning dirt
from its round loaf. Grandpa died at 96—
I'd outgrown him at 12. Turning back, finding grief
answers the knock, the knock of his awkward box.
Grandpa, these two old grackles were once your girls:
guard them by your shop's infinite mirrors—*tick*

tick tick tick—the tail end of tape whirls around
the recorder's flat breast; snippets, hellos, songs
unfurl like your own full last name: Bleishewitz.

Push Play

The driveway slab lay like a tongue depressor
between my room and the sour, harassed boy's;
at six I heard him scrape his bedroom dresser
against the door and yell *Bull.* Now he toys

with his TV, his face glazed the calm blue
of a window-saint. Lately he's been mumbling
backtalk to himself—it's all he can do:
when his cute mom pecks, or her drug-puffed, stumbling

boyfriend harangues him, he mouths a quiet pledge.
No friends come home, but he keeps pets until
they bore him—a hamster, lost in the hedge;
ants ate the bees. One "pet" dropped to his sill,

a puny-winged hysteric which his cat
worried over. He held it in the yard
while its freckly mom flailed at him or sat
crabbing from the gutters. Her pleas were hard,

like a hinge cackling when a child would swing
a door back and forth for fun . . . and this child
played her, he conducted her suffering
with the dying chick in his hands. Mild

and curious, he recorded their duet
"for my school report" he explained to me
after we buried the soft chick. And yet
he kept on playing it till dinner, and she

flew back each time to wail. I couldn't read,
hearing my own plot each time he pushed PLAY,
knowing he made her hostage in his greed,
hating his joy. Her nest complained all day—

but she advised the box that voices came from.
The chick stops replying. She hears her own hoarse
call, scolds it, and then the boy. He looks glum
watching her fly home till he pushes REVERSE.

Leopard Man

Mom once posed as LaGuardia's girlfriend
and smoothed her way past an usher.
She gets gas-attacks at lectures,
   and even gave
herself a cardiac, worrying which cruise

to take. A lifelong scrimmage between
ambition and self-doubt has given her
a fretful, pestering energy, and a genius
   for quirky triumphs
over cabbie, onion, and varicose vein.

Working in a museum gift shop
she hears that Reagan has been shot,
and says, "Hinckley botched the job."
   Was it that,
or was it her rebuking letters—each one

signed *An ex-Republican* so it hurt more?
—Something put her on a list. Because
a Secret Serviceman comes to question her;
   No sunglasses now,
he's undercover, and checking his notes:

"*Young Spartacus. Gray Panther.* Quote:
'I'd wear a dynamite girdle and blow
us both up. They'd never check me—
    I'm a grandma.'"
The bronze breasts of an Ethiopian Goddess

almost touch his back—he doesn't see them,
but I do, generations of schoolboys
have rubbed her cool nipples all shiny:
    big golden pawns.
And I love to see my mother behind

the counter, tidying up the fossil fish
and reptile rulers, watching him walk up,
and whispering a sales blessing on the lot—
    a wizard of retail.
He fingers some shark's teeth, chatting

headlines, politics: "Yeah, and what about
his cutback on Aid to Dependent Children. . . ."
"He's a stinking lousy miser, that's what.
    This talking drum,
see it? and the husk face—both on sale."

Back and forth they go—he, schooled in
Interview Maneuvers; she, assuming a man
so full of grudges would want a bargain.
    "So tell me,
what should we do about a man like that?"

We've all heard Mom blurt out *Assassination*
in answer to this. Now she muses, "Do?
Well, I don't know. . . . I guess we could
    vote him out
of office. . .?" Which sends him packing,

while Mom sits and rests her ankles,
safe within her Old Testament justice
and shopkeeper's courtesy. Encased nearby,
    the Leopard Man
has seen all this. The Leopard Man,

exorcist of his tribe while he wears
the skin, who could suffer a vision
and kill his whole family, and yet
    be spared because
in dreams he sees the enemy clearly.

He stoops behind the glass, a fusty
mannequin—one eye points at Mom, but
the other is painted too far to the side;
    his sight widens,
and the world could fall within his gaze.

Last Garden

—my father's stroke

Survey of your eye

Spectral lily, trickle of phosphorus,
blood-midge and polyp, salt lace
nursed in pus—
a garden of disease
stained on the inkpress glass;
last garden, grown in its health
by the specimen-patient.

Between your eyepiece and your eye
a play of reflections . . .
your eye felt no play.
Yet cords behind it tingled,
brain-wall soaked and informed—
name, condition, and source you knew,
clamping the jags in a gummy cure;
holy knowledge, that would lift
a man from his sickbed.

Your vision

Under the memory-quilt, patched
by the splintered family,
under the roof of nights
hushing the risen

crossword puzzles of ink,
Whan that April from college,
the chambered multitudes of death
studied and preserved—
your mind's
fabulous catacomb, built
"Because education is the only thing
they can't take from us—"

It was not "they" who came—
not death slid under your eye,
you did not recognize. . . .

Those who watched the miracle
of falling bread, asking *manna*—
The desert-man, asked the name of
the jumping beast, *kangaroo*—

. . . these things without names,
names of not-know,
Manna what is it
Kangaroo don't know—
new creations, Adam didn't see them. . . .

Nor could you see what
passed through
your sleeping eye,
what held its reasons behind
your eye
and drilled the brain stock.
You were struck,
and woke like a visionary.

Dr. Johnson's prayer

His learning was supreme and brought him fear,
rolling down the hill from heaven to hell.
Mammoth at table, he grumbled about
"the Infidel Hume," but preferred to call him *I;*

and wondered if the boy cured of blindness
would understand a triangle.
Then, a stroke:

". . . I felt a confusion and
indistinctness in my head . . . prayed God
that however He might afflict my body
He would spare my understanding."

—This he prayed in Latin,
but knew the lines were bad.
"I . . . concluded myself to be
unimpaired in my faculties."

Dying later, he asked his doctor
Macbeth's question,
"Can you not minister to a mind diseased?"

And the doctor,
"Therein the patient must
minister to himself."

Your Fugitives

. . . Wincing, sluggish, bewildered,
morning light voided black-blank
on the cornea, your sight
thick with hallucinations—

as if the scorched
occipital nerve had
electrocuted your corpses
back to life, as if
they bolted from the cooled
wards of cerebra
and poured out of your eye—

"For two days I was seeing
dead people walking round the room"
—old familiars, wearing
the medals of disease
while you chatted with your dead mom
and frightened wife.

You could not treat yourself—
driving lost a hundred miles,
names of your family lost—
could not read the *Manual of Symptoms*
or see a doctor, pride demanding that
you know the diagnosis first—
Sickness cleansed your mind of its name,
your hapless will calling
what what what
from a citadel of necros—

Your changes

A nightmare only sleep would end.
Then rest, and wanderings through your house,
the temple of knick-knack.
Forced at last to the hospital,
half-blind before a staff of youngsters,
suddenly, this opening gift—
you said please, and listened to your doctors;

you kissed your wife, learned to read
again, didn't trust yourself—
No driving. No moat of gin.
Patient, hopeful, half-surrendering,
impish, caring, forgetful, shaken—
your daughter, whom you loved
over your shoulder,
cried hearing you praise her at last.

Gone is your genius in forestalling deaths:
nature recovers its mysteries,
and leaves you only your death.
You seem strangely distracted,
as if working out another problem;

tired now and crumbling,
rawly incomplete, you've turned
toward a puzzle long deferred,
holding it with ignorance and with grace—
this masterful late imperfect love.

Tribute

I leapt up in my sleep
again they come
forms of cadavers
my father has entered
crackling the papers
crumpled by the bed

Each held what killed it
for me to inscribe
I learned the final causes
tumor clots a child a knife
I fell down sleeping

What I do and cannot do is one gesture

At dawn I tasted print
smeared across the pages.

The Fossil

I replaced the word "God" everywhere with "Sculpture," and it worked, and it was right.

—Rodin

In the beginning, God yearned for bodies:
they kept leaving Him, all but the statues,
   who now reign

massive, inert, as we whisper their names
like a family watching the deathbed.
  Stone Guest:

To stand like that—untouched, waiting for
the restorer—not this gaping hollow.
   We cherish statues

for seeming human, or for bearing
human marks, Giacometti's fingerprints
   blurred on

muscles he pinched off, that his brother
smoothed back each night like Penelope, the
   raked and moistened

surfaces regenerate as flesh. But they watch us
warily: our slackness and decay. . . .
   Sculptures

were born on the eighth day, when loss appeared
in the world; for them, that day never ends—
    they attend us

like messengers forgetful of their charge,
and comfort each other in museums at night,
    or in parks

where Queen Victoria busts are stored, circled in
perfect council, a lime-streaked necropolis of one
    self-regarding

absence. In the movie, statues follow The Beast
with their eyes—his unsettled flesh, bristles and
    nails surging out

or sinking back when he faces Beauty.
How careless this new god is, skittish,
    disturbing—

And yet, in their hell-day of creation,
hands like his had sealed the statues up—
    had soldered

a mold of Laocoön and his sons,
till they stood fretted by the godly snakes,
    and by pipes

through which the metals pour. Inside
that chamber, a gloomy family of air
    waits. . . .

The bronze puddles in and they hiss upward,
breath of change dissolving in the room—
   whose door

is shut, the models gone home, the work,
like a fossil from God, baked, coffined,
   ignored, and still.

Notes

"Annals of the Wonder-Cabinet": the "Texas Mix" used is sodium pentithol, Parulon, and potassium chloride. "Dr. Fleming": penicillin wafting through air vents infested Alexander Fleming's petri dishes; he did not understand its medical potential at first.

"Catalunya: A Letter": set in Barcelona, when Colonel Tejero seized the Parliament (February 23, 1981). *"Cátala, Catalunya"*—the native language and name of Catalonia.

"Leg-of-Mutton Pond": Caligula attacked Neptune in this Richmond Park pond, according to local tradition.